sp
PET

CATS

by Mari Schuh

AMICUS | AMICUS INK

whiskers

tail

Look for these words and pictures as you read.

claws

tongue

Meow! Meow!
A cat wants to play.

Cats are fun pets.
Male cats are called toms.
Female cats are called queens.

Do you see its whiskers?
They are long.
They help cats feel things.

whiskers

tail

Do you see its tail?

It is high in the air.

That means the cat is curious.

claws

Do you see its claws?

Cats scratch things.

Scratching keeps claws healthy.

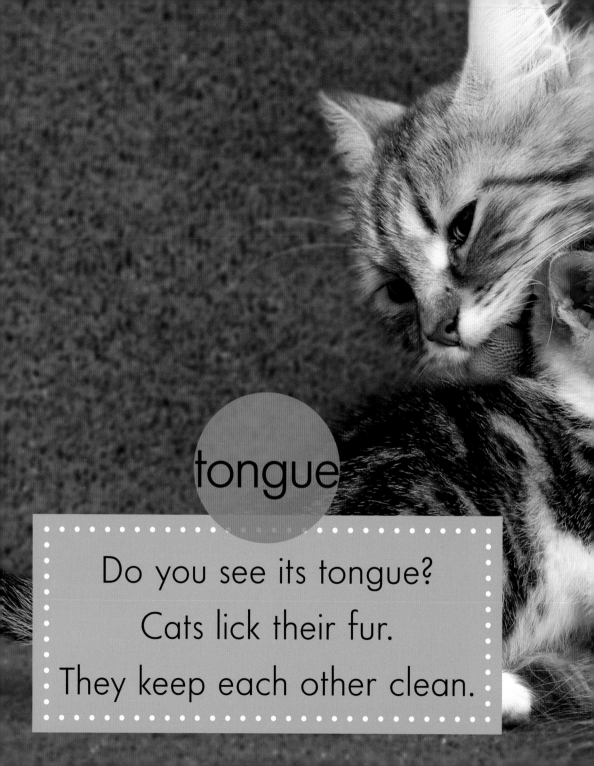

tongue

Do you see its tongue?
Cats lick their fur.
They keep each other clean.

A cat rests.
It is warm and calm.
It purrs.

Do you see its whiskers?
They are long.
They help cats feel things.

whiskers

tail

Do you see its tail?
It is high in the air.
That means the cat is curious.

whiskers

tail

Did you
find?

claws

tongue

claws

Do you see its claws?
Cats scratch.
Scratching keeps claws health.

tongue

Do you see its tongue?
Cats lick their fur.
They keep each other clean.

spot

Spot is published by Amicus and Amicus Ink
P.O. Box 1329, Mankato, MN 56002
www.amicuspublishing.us

Library of Congress Cataloging-in-Publication Data
Names: Schuh, Mari C., 1975- author.
Title: Cats / by Mari Schuh.
Description: Mankato, Minnesota : Amicus, [2019] | Series:
Spot. Pets | Audience: K to grade 3.
Identifiers: LCCN 2017029531 (print) | LCCN 2017030016
  (ebook) | ISBN 9781681514475 (ebook) | ISBN
  9781681513652 (library bound) | ISBN 9781681522852
  (paperback)
Subjects: LCSH: Cats--Juvenile literature. | CYAC: Cats. |
  Pets.
Classification: LCC SF445.7 (ebook) | LCC SF445.7 .S354
  2019 (print) | DDC 636.8--dc23
LC record available at https://lccn.loc.gov/2017029531

Printed in China

HC 10 9 8 7 6 5 4 3 2 1
PB 10 9 8 7 6 5 4 3 2 1

For Nan —MS

Wendy Dieker, editor
Deb Miner, series designer
Ciara Beitlich, book designer
Holly Young, photo researcher

Photos by Alamy 8–9, 10–11, 14–15;
Dreamstime 1, iStock 3, 4–5, 6–7,
Shutterstock cover, 12–13

CATS